HASHTAGS FOR DAILY LIVING

Postive Affirming Thoughts to
Brighten Your Day

Debbie George

Authentic Deb Publications

Copyright © 2020 Debbie George

All rights reserved

The characters and events portrayed in this book are fictitious. Any similarity to real persons, living or dead, is coincidental and not intended by the author.

Photo Design by: Debbie George
Bus Photo Credit to Sharon Wright via https://unsplash.com/@shasha333

No part of this book may be reproduced, or stored in a retrieval system, or transmitted in any form or by any means, electronic, mechanical, photocopying, recording, or otherwise, without express written permission of the publisher.

ISBN-9798657480535

Cover design by: Art Painter
Library of Congress Control Number: 2018675309
Printed in the United States of America

Have you ever had a vision that seemed so big, so exciting that you stopped yourself before even trying?

That was me before I had a mindset shift and met several freaking amazing people who kicked my butt (in tough love) to the moon and back. We all need those kinds of people who demand us to live the extraordinary lives we were created to live. Who are these fantastic lightworkers who have impacted my life so significantly? Just some of the most amazing people in the entire universe! I'll be sharing why they are so amazing throughout my journey, suffice it to say, I am one blessed girl with so many amazing people in my life.

This HashTag Book is dedicated to the awesome people who helped me see my gifts and have never given up on me.

Moea, Letty, Mallory, Lisa (AKA Ella) Jell-O Joe, Anke, Diane, Marion, Cindy, Gali and Laurie
just to name a few of my awesome tribe.

Mom, Dad, Keith, Ben (Number One Son) CiCI (Number One Daughter in Love)

My Awesome Wife Susan, The one great Love of my Life. Life is Sweet with you in it. I don't know how you put up with me, but glad that you do!

My God. Every single good thing about me comes from you!

CONTENTS

Title Page	
Copyright	
Dedication	
Introduction:	1
#DoYou	2
#Authentic	3
#BeNice	4
#Challenges	7
#Dream Big	8
#EnjoytheJourney	9
#FindYourVoice	10
#Focus	11
#FreakingAwesome	12
#IAmEnough	13
#IGotYou	14
#KeepMoving	15
#Launch	16
#LiveintheNow	17
#LoveSaysYes	18
#Move	19
#Permission	21

#Questions	22
#StartingOver	24
#VibeHigh	25
#WhatIf	26
Thank you	29

INTRODUCTION:

This collection of Hashtags has gone through many changes as I struggled with Ms. Perfect rearing her Barbie Blonde Head in my face every step along the way. I have written and erased this little collection so often; it became apparent that my desire to make the perfect ebook on my first attempt was sucking all the fun and life out of me.

So instead of trying to make every entry uniformed, I present to you my thoughts on any given day. Some entries are long; some are short. Some have a declaration at the end; others don't. I decided that I cannot very well be Authentic Deb if I am forcing myself into a box of how my thoughts are conveyed. With that, I pray that the entries you find here will uplift you, make you laugh, give you food for thought and encourage you never to give up. And most of all, remember...

Be You, Because Being You is Enough.

Enjoy the Journey!

Authentic Deb

#DOYOU

I choose this hashtag for the first entry in my book because it represents something special for me.

Can you relate to what I am saying? It has taken me years to love myself enough to work on self-acceptance. To express who I fully am in all my quirkiness, strengths, and weaknesses. And while I would be lying if I said that I did not want to be understood, the truth is that not everyone is going to get me, or even like me.

So while I am mindful to keep the law of love at the forefront of everything I do, I have come to the marvelous conclusion just to be myself. And so fellow sojourners, I invite you on this wild, crazy, spectacular journey called life. Be You, Do You, regardless of who gets you.

Do You - Because Being You is Enough!
And besides, it's exhausting to try to be someone else.
Who has time for that?

#AUTHENTIC

One of my favorite words! I've based my life and the name of my business on it. While I am a naturally outgoing person and super authentic and transparent, I would be lying if I said Authenticity is not something that I have had to work out over the years. Some of the definitions of Authentic are as follows.

- Not false or copied
- Genuine and real
- Being and acting as who you claim to be
- Our qualities and conduct towards others are in accord with what we genuinely believe

Do you or your friends resemble any of these examples?

I challenge you today, to look inward and see where you can make some changes. The more I free myself to be authentic, the happier and more joyful my life has become.

#BENICE

I am writing this hashtag during the Covid19 crisis, and I am both encouraged and somewhat dismayed by the actions and thoughts of others. It amazes me how self-centered we act as a human race. The world is hurting, the planet is diseased, and people all over the world are hurting. Covid19 does not care about race, creed, religion, color, age, or sexuality.

We, the human race, are so profoundly divided about every issue, and this pandemic has brought out the best and worst of people. As I write this, I am sitting at our country house watching the trees wave in the wind and the occasional bunny outside my window, and it's beautiful. It's peaceful. The serenity of where I am at, in my little bubble, gives me hope for the world. There is no stress here, and there is no jealousy here, there is no chaos in this place. No one is yelling or screaming for their rights, and there is no political party out here in the county.

There is so much good in the world; we are capable of raising the vibration of the world. To be light, to shine the light, and to walk as one who exudes love wherever they go.

I challenge you to walk in love. Be Nice, Be Kind. You know being friendly and kind does not mean you agree with everything going in the world. But do we have to put people down, demean them, or spew out our hate so much on the internet?

Remember that you get what you give. We are what we think, and words have power. When I think happy thoughts, everything around me changes. Yes, it is that simple.

Be Nice - You Get What You Give.

#Brave

A couple of years ago, I started choosing a word to live by for the calendar year. This word Brave was the first word I wanted. I had many words floating around in my head that I could have used. Ultimately, I chose this word because it exemplified everything I was and everything I hoped to be. I allowed myself to throw out the negative thinking of why I might not resemble this word, or walk it out day to day. What I found to be right for me and I pray it resonates with you is this. "Bravery is a continuous act of showing courage under the face of extreme pressure or doubts." That is the Authentic Deb definition and not Websters. The dictionary says this.

- Ready to face and endure danger or pain; showing courage.
- Endure or face (unpleasant conditions or behavior) without showing fear.

I know that I am Brave, as I am confident you are whether you feel it to be true or not. I like my definition of Brave because I make a choice every day to wake up and live my life in a way that feels the most authentic to me. That means that there are times I have no idea what I am doing, but I do it anyway. I have times of extreme doubt about my abilities to learn new things or accomplish a project. I go for it anyways.

I continue to take my thoughts captive, and when they are full of what I like to call "Stinking Thinking," I replace them with positive thoughts that fuel me to keep going. I am not perfect, this book is not perfect, and I still have doubts and fears like all of you. I do, however, have an intense desire to face my fears and do it anyway.

So yeah, I'm Brave, and so are you!

#CHALLENGES

Recently, I have been pondering about the different seasons in my life and how each season brings its own set of challenges. Have you ever noticed that anything worth doing is worth doing well? I have found that the things I have struggled the most with are those things that bring the most fulfillment and joy to me when accomplished.

While I'm not the type to back away from a challenge, I can experience a healthy dose of fear, doubt, or trepidation going on inside my head where the battleground lies.

Every day we have a choice to step into what your heart is desiring or sit on the couch and hope our dreams magically appear. You can stay comfortable, stay with the status quo, and never release the greatness within you, or you can strap on your climbing gear and get up that mountain. It may take days, weeks, or even years to get to the finish line, but I promise you it will be worth it.

I double dog dare you to try something new!

#DREAM BIG

Have you ever had a dream that was so huge that you managed to talk yourself out of it before you even started? I see so much into the future with the vision that I have and get all excited and then find myself trying to figure out how to make it all happen.

In the past, this has resulted in a wasteland of unfulfilled dreams. They have gone out to what I call "The valley of unfulfilled dreams and desires." Do you have a valley of unfulfilled desires in your landscape? Did you convince yourself that your vision too big, too scary, cost too much money, or any other plethora of excuses we can manufacture?

It's time to breathe on your dreams and resurrect them.

Ask God to bring all the people and tools you need in your life to bring your vision into reality. You will get there if you don't quit! So for today, breathe deep, close your eyes, and Dream Big! Remember that Dream plus Action = Reality and Manifestation!

Declare: I breathe life into my dreams and desires. As I move forward, I will see my dreams manifest into reality.

#ENJOYTHEJOURNEY

Often, I have heard the statement, "It's not where you start; it's where you finish." As someone who has taken many unexpected twists and turns on my journey, I understand the intent behind that statement. What I have noticed is that at points in my life, I have been so focused on getting from one place to the other, that I have not stopped to smell the roses along the way. In my quest for the destination, I have metaphorically held my breath with a tunnel-like vision to get from point A to point B. Once there, I breathe and allow myself to enjoy my surroundings. I can tell you that my "Just get there" mentality has not served me one iota.

The older and wiser I get, the more I see the beauty of life all around me. What we would call the good, the bad, and the ugly is all around me, and each step on my journey is worthy of stopping to explore, identify, learn and relish along the way. Life is not like the Indy 500, with drivers going in circles as fast as they can. Yet, we tend to treat our life that way at times. Have you fallen prey to this thought of "Just get there?" I know I have been in that state of mind many times. The joy I have found in living in the moment is the pleasure of enjoying the journey. All parts of my journey are adding to my life experience. They are my teachers, my encouragers, my course correctors if you will. Today, I invite you to #EnjoytheJourney with me. By the time you reach your destination, you will be able to sit back and say, "Woo, what a ride!."

Declare: My life is an incredible journey!

#FINDYOURVOICE

How many times have we not expressed what we were thinking because of the opinions of others? We stay silent in meetings, say yes when we mean no, and otherwise limit ourselves. Did you know that people need to hear what it is you have to say? You, yes You! Life's too short to be concerned with how many people agree with or even understand you.

What matters is that you were placed here in this time and space for a unique purpose. Your voice is needed to help raise the vibrations of the earth. So, stand up, hold your head high, and say what you have to say. You can speak it, draw it, sing it, write it, create it. There are no limits to how you share your voice with the world. We just need to hear it so speak up and #FindYourVoice.

Need Help Finding Your Voice? Contact Authentic Deb for a free 15-minute session.

#FOCUS

What do you think of when you hear or read the word focus? Are you thinking about bringing your mind back to the task at hand? Did you think about your glasses or contacts that you are wearing, or was your mind wandering? There are many ways that we can lose our focus and have to regroup. Sometimes our perception is off-target because we are not using the right lens for that moment. No matter how hard you try, constant attention on any goal can be elusive at best. Yet the ability to focus is vital to living our life in our way and on our terms.

If you don't zero in and get real with what you are focusing on, many others will try to step in and offer their perspective. People who do not have your vision will usually be more comfortable if you focus through their lens, so it is vital to guard your focus, keep it pure, wipe your eyes, and make sure you are heading in the direction you intended to go.

Stay true to yourself and follow your vision only!

#FREAKINGAWESOME

How often do we take the time to consider just how valuable we are to the world around us? It is so easy to see the good in others and express to them how much we value them, but what about you?

When was the last time you told yourself that you are Freaking Awesome?

You are an intricate piece of this puzzle we call life, and the world around us is not the same without the uniqueness that you bring to it. We need your laughter, wisdom, and your presence to make our world a better place. So today, my Authentic friends, I want to be the first to tell you that you are #FreakingAwsome, I mean, you are the cream of the crop, the bee's knees, all that and then some!

Declare: I am Freaking Awesome, and the world needs my light.

#IAMENOUGH

I Am Enough, three small words that pack a lot of power. We live in a world that is continuously telling us how limited we are. We are told we are not young enough, old enough, thin enough, smart enough, or rich enough. As I was musing on this, I had a vision of a maze. I saw all the different turns, dead ends, and confusing circles that you find in any puzzle, and then I saw the words "I Am Enough." These words were blinking brightly in my vision, shouting for me to peer into their message. You see, a traditional maze has many dead ends before you reach the finish line.

What if we looked at the maze we call life differently? What if this maze has the affirmation, "I Am Enough" displayed at every turn and every dead end.

What would that do to your confidence? How would that raise your Vibration? Life is a constant discovery of who we are, what we want, and the many paths we take: and the lessons we learned along the way.

I challenge you today to celebrate every single path.

You Are Enough right here and right now wherever you are.

#IGOTYOU

I have been thinking about true friendship lately and wanted to share an old journal entry. Have you ever heard the analogy about your circle of friends? You have a big circle of acquaintances, then a smaller inner circle and finally one or two people that are your closest confidants. While we all long for relationships, I believe it is vital to have those #IGotyou types of friends in our life. So, who are your #IGotYou friends? How do we identify them and lastly, are you that type of friend for someone else? We need to know that there are people in our life that have our backs no matter what, and will hold up our arms when we're too tired to lift them.

These friends are the ones that pick you up. They sit with you in silence when there are no answers to be found. They cry with you when the emotion must come out, and they laugh with you and rejoice with you. They're the ones that are pushing you into greater things. They believe in you. They speak life and agreement into your potential and into your dreams. These types of friends form a circle of strength around you. They challenge you; they tell you the truth, and they love to see you succeed. They not only get you, but they also got you.

And so Hashtag #IGotYou.

Who you Got Today?

#KEEPMOVING

Have you ever had a great idea, and then you just ran out of steam? You wrote out the vision, you made plans, set some things in motion, and you were on top of the world, and then something happens. Maybe work got busy, and the kids got sick, the bills go huge. So many things in life can creep up to derail us right as we were in the grove of making progress.

I have played the victim to this more times than I can count. I am pretty sure I would be a millionaire by now if I had just followed through on some of those divine downloads I received for business ideas. Today we can make a decision together to #KeepMoving. No more sitting in the ruts of our past, wondering how life passed you up. Take today by the horns and go for it.

Get back up, Dust off that manuscript, put your eyes back on the vision, and get to work. You may not be where you want to be, but I promise you this one thing, if you just #KeepMoving, you're going to get somewhere and have a lot of fun learning along the way.

I challenge you to turn off the TV and get back in the game!

#LAUNCH

Have you ever had a great idea or goal in mind, and you feel the excitement in your bones, and then months later, you're still sitting on that idea? If this is you, don't fret, you are not alone! I have experienced these failure to launch issues more times than I'd like to admit. Take this book you are reading now. The idea for this book came in 2016, and here it is three years later before I pulled up my big girl panties and started writing.

What holds us back from launching into new things?

Speaking for myself alone, I would say mindset on what I believe about myself and the world around me has had everything to do with how long it has taken me to launch out into the unknown. You see, I can be a bit of a control freak and like to know the end before the beginning. Failure to launch based on fear of the unknown has never served me, and it does not help you either.

So, today friends, I challenge you to #Launch.
Take your dream or your goal and "Set it in Motion."

Release what is holding you back and be true to yourself first.

Your dreams, goals, and purpose are right around the corner, waiting for you to Launch!

#LIVEINTHENOW

Living joyfully has been a struggle for me recently. Every step forward, sent me two steps back; the fear of making the same mistakes of the past was constant on my mind and hindering me from starting over. And then, in a time where I felt most alone, I heard the voice of Spirit say to me, "Live in the Now."

Living in the now frees me from the pain of the past and enables me to jump exuberantly into today.

I have chosen to be present now. As I breathe, I feel the energy of the Spirit filling my lungs, fueling every part of me with new possibilities. Have you been mired in the past? I invite you to heal with me and Live in the Now. Today is a gift, breathe it in, embrace it and Live!

I learned to breathe again, to trust my intuition, and to trust others.

Today I am grateful for life. I have vision, love, shelter, health, and sustenance. Everything I need, I have right here and right now. At this moment, in this time and space, I am "Living in the Now."

Take a deep breath and ask yourself what space you're living in?

#LOVESAYSYES

Love is the Universal Law that holds everything else together. To vibrate at the frequency of Love can and will overshadow all lower frequencies. Love; pure, simple, and profound Love heals. Love opens the heart of others to live their best life. Love encourages, Love says I believe in you, Love knows you can do it. Love never gives up and doesn't judge by first impressions.

Love says yes to all possibilities. It says yes to all people for it knows the power and potential in each human soul. Out of all the words you say today, try on Love. Love Says Yes, Yes you can, Yes you will, Yes you are forgiven, Yes I will help you, Yes I will walk through this season with you. Let your voice express Love today in whatever shape and form it comes in.

When you operate in Love, you are a helper and a healer in this world. You are declaring that you will be a voice of reason and solution, rather than the sound of dissent. It means that you filter everything you do through this pivotal universal law of Love. Love hopes all, believes all, sees all, is all. Without Love operating in our lives, we will not fully be alive the way our mind body and souls were intended

I challenge you today to up your Love Game. Start with loving yourself and then spread it around!

#MOVE

You have heard it said before that for your dreams to manifest, action is needed. Many times, I have taken steps on a great idea, and then I stopped before seeing it come to fruition. I can say with absolute certainty that *if you stop moving, you will stay exactly where you are*.

Oh, I know what you're thinking, "Debbie, you're so brilliant and profound!" why thank you, but you know it's true. Sometimes, we need to stop, look, and listen for the next step.

There are several reasons we stop moving.

- We are stuck in fear- IE, False Evidence Appearing Real
- We are out of gas, spiritually, physically, emotionally
- We are waiting for something or someone to finish a task before we can go forward.

While rest periods are necessary, like pit stops at a racetrack, we often tend to park our vision. Instead, let's fuel up and get back in the race. Movement keeps your dream alive and pushes you towards the finish line. Any positive change is a step taken toward your goal, so get up, dust off, fuel up, and get moving!

Declare: I take the rest I need and get back in the race.

#NeverAlone

I wrote a song that ends with the words, "I am never alone."

How many times have we felt all alone and found ourselves in despair and holding onto pain because we have been isolated from our family and friends? We feel alone in our circumstances and cannot see a way out of the situation. I have often caught myself sitting in my condition with my mind twirling in a hundred directions and have found myself getting more frustrated with every moment that goes by, and then I remember to call out to the Lord. My favorite prayer is a straightforward one.

"HELP LORD!" The clouds roll back from my mind, and peace enters my heart when I say these simple words.

We are truly never alone, God says he will not leave you or turn his back on you. He wants us to know that He is always close to us. He sees all, He hears all, and He knows all our concerns. When we remind ourselves that God is intimately concerned with what concerns us, we can take comfort in knowing the authentic presence of God himself.

Right now, where you are, just remind yourself that you are Truly Never Alone! Let the peace of God fill you today wherever you are, whatever your situation.

God, Your word says you are with me wherever I go. I need your peace today. Open my heart to know your presence today. I am Never alone!

#PERMISSION

Have you ever talked yourself out of finishing a project or perhaps never starting one at all because you set limits on yourself?

Have you ever worked so hard that you ran yourself ragged, and now it feels like walking through mud to get to the finish line?

Why do I ask?

I ask because if you're anything like me, you resonate with at least one, if not all, of these statements.

I challenge you to give yourself **#Permission** to be who you are and where you are right now at this moment.

The key is to permit yourself to accept and honor how you feel at any given time. If you have overextended yourself, then be kind to yourself and rest. Saying no is not the end of the world, and stopping to rest will gain you some much-needed peace and serenity.

Declare with me:

Today I give myself permission to take care of myself, body, soul, and spirit.

#QUESTIONS

Today I want you to ponder with me for a moment the freedom that comes with allowing yourself to ask questions. How many times have you chosen to hold back a question out of fear of the opinions of others?

Failing to ask questions or request clarification on an issue out of fear of how you may be perceived is based on fear. We might not want to call it that but let us think about it for a moment. If you don't ask the question, then you walk away, denying that inner part of yourself that wanted clarity.

And that feels crappy. What is the worst that can happen? Someone laughs at you or thinks you were not paying attention. So what? Maybe you were not paying attention, ask the question, and move forward.

Sometimes we don't ask the question. After all, we have this fear that people would judge us because we should already know the answer.

That is a load of BS. I encourage you to fire "Should Have, Could Have, Would Have" out of your vocabulary. But that is for another Hashtag entry.

Allow yourself the freedom to embrace who you are fully and take off the limits of what is acceptable to ask. Many questions are running around in your head, whether they are for someone or God, or a situation. Whatever it is, questions are right. Questions allow the way for us to have the answers and direction we are seeking. So my Authentic Friends. Do your soul a favor and ask the questions that are rumbling around in your heart to ask. Others don't have to understand you, as long as you are empowering yourself just to be you.

#Show up

While social media is a powerful tool to connect us with friends and loved ones in different states and countries, it should not take the place of in-person interaction. How many people do you text daily that live within distance for you to visit? There is a beautiful healing power in human interaction, in a hug, in a smile, and something incredibly powerful and healing in being there for someone.

Ask your inner voice, who you need to Show Up for today, and then go and be the bright light that you are!

#STARTINGOVER

If you're anything like me, I am sure you have several projects that you have started and never finished.

Recently I have been picking up old projects that I had let fall to the wayside for various reasons. They felt like the most fabulous ideas on the planet at the time. I was sure it would launch me into stardom and riches, I let my imagination run wild with all the things I could accomplish.

I don't know what changed for me to stop working on them. I suppose it was the day to day process of life, and the day to day responsibilities that we all experience. Life, while a grand adventure, comes with its own unique sets of challenges daily. It's easy to get bogged down in the routine and put our dreams and projects to the side in place of laundry, dishes, kids, work, or whatever other superpowers you have.

Here is what I have found to be right for me in this season, and I hope it encourages you to do the same. Pick back up the projects that bring you joy. Let go of the grandiose outcome you envisioned (Speaking to myself here) and start over, or pick up where you left off. Take off all the restrictions and go for it.

These might not be the most profound words you have ever written, but then again, the truth remains. Do what makes you happy, permit yourself to start over.

Let your vision reshape itself and have fun with it.

#VIBEHIGH

Did you know that everything in creation has a frequency? Has a vibration? Have you ever walked into a room full of people and felt your mood instantly drop or just felt off? Or perhaps you had walked into a crowded and immediately felt lighter, better, happier than when you walked in. We could talk about Empaths and how they pick up on others' feelings, but that's for another HashTag!

Everything you see has a vibration, including you. Lower vibrations tend to bring us down, cause motion sickness and other unwanted feelings. Higher vibrations can make you feel "Lighter" and are suitable for your physical, emotional, and mental bodies. It's much easier to gain clarity and have peace about a situation when you are at a High Vibe rather than when you are down.

Today, be the Thermostat and not the Thermometer. Change your mindset and #VibeHigh

#WHATIF

When I was a younger adult, I had a pastor tell me that I was the queen of the "What If's." It was not a statement meant to encourage me; instead, it was said in exasperation because, at least in her mind, I was full of doubt and fear and had a reason for absolutely everything that could go wrong. At the time, I was slightly embarrassed by her perception of who I was as a person. I did not agree with ALL of it, yet there was some truth to her statement.

I challenge you with #WhatIF.

- What if it all goes right?
- What if you are the right person for the job?
- What if you succeed?
- What if you risk and write that book,
- Start the business,
- Put yourself out there?

So many questions, and only one way to find out!

THANK YOU

Hey Authentic Friends! That's all for now, but I will update more entries to this collection and email you when revisions come out. Remember what I said at the beginning that I had to Fire Ms. Perfect and move some action to my vision, else we would not even be this far.

I so appreciate you taking the time to read my little musings. I pray that you read something that resonated with you at just the right time and place.

For notices of new entries to this HashTag journal make sure to head on over to my AuthenticDeb Website to join my mailing list. Don't worry about endless emails or spam. I am a busy girl with a full time job, who has no energy to email you every day or show you pictures of my food on facebook. Spam? No Way! I'm just to Freaking Amazing to sell your address.

I would love to connect with you. You can find me For all things Authentic, from coaching, online courses, and more head on over to my Authentic Deb website.